Let's Play

Games Around the World

By Tami B. Morton

CELEBRATION PRESS
Pearson Learning Group

Contents

Getting Ready to Play

Hooray for games! In this book you'll learn how to play games from five different countries. Before you play each game, read the directions carefully. Make sure you have all the things listed in the What You Need box. Then start playing!

Learn how to play Shagai on page 6.

Ampe

Ampe (AM-peh) is a jumping game that's fun for everyone. Two players play at a time. In Ghana one player is called Ohyiwa (OH-yee-wah). The other is called Opare (OH-pah-ree).

What You Need

- two players
- music

How to Play Ampe

1 Decide who is Ohyiwa and who is Opare. When both players are ready, start the music.

2 Together clap to the beat.

3 After four claps jump up. As you land, choose a foot to kick out. Freeze with that foot up.

4 If both players kick the same leg, Opare wins a point. If players kick different legs, Ohyiwa wins a point. The first player to get ten points wins the game.

Scoring

Ohyiwa   **Opare**

Players kicked the same leg. Opare gets a point.

Ohyiwa   **Opare**

Players kicked different legs. Ohyiwa gets a point.

Shagai

Children in Mongolia play with game pieces made from sheep anklebones. In the Mongolian language, the bones are called shagai (sha-GY). The game here is a form of one Mongolian game played with shagai. Instead of real shagai, you use dice.

What You Need

- two or more players

- dice (Use ten dice if two players are playing. Add five dice for each player added to the game.)

- one extra dice for each player

- a large, flat surface (like a tabletop or a floor)

Shagai Bones

A real shagai has four sides. Mongolian people use shagai to play many different games.

How to Play Shagai

1 Decide who goes first. Give each player one dice to keep. Then roll the rest of the dice onto the flat surface.

2 On each turn, find two dice with the same number of dots showing. Use your own dice to hit one of the dice in the pair, without touching any other dice.

3 If you hit a dice correctly, you get to keep it. Then look for another pair and try to hit one of those dice. If you miss, your turn is over.

4 Players take turns until there are no more matching dice pairs. Whoever has the most dice at the end of the game wins.

Jan, Ken, Pon

In many parts of the world, this game is known as Rock, Paper, Scissors. Two people can play the game anywhere. You don't need a game board or any other items. All you need is a friend willing to play.

What You Need

- two players

These players' hands are in the paper and rock shapes. Paper wins this round.

Hand Positions

rock (a fist)

paper (a flat hand)

scissors (two fingers)

How to Play Jan, Ken, Pon

1 Sit facing the other player.

2 Hold out your hands in fists. Move your fists up and down as you say, "Jan, ken, pon."

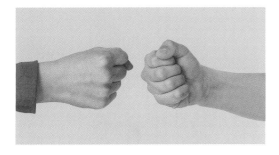

3 As you say "pon," quickly move your hands into one of the three shapes (rock, paper, or scissors). The box on the right shows who wins the round.

4 Give a point to the winner of the round and play again. The first player with ten points wins the game.

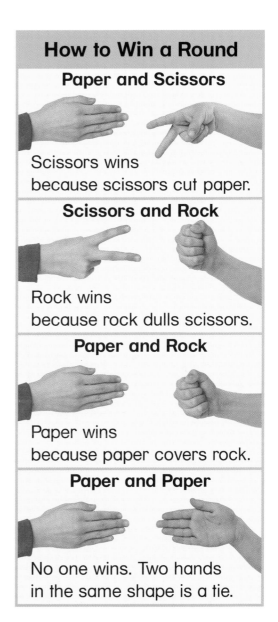

How to Win a Round

Paper and Scissors

Scissors wins
because scissors cut paper.

Scissors and Rock

Rock wins
because rock dulls scissors.

Paper and Rock

Paper wins
because paper covers rock.

Paper and Paper

No one wins. Two hands
in the same shape is a tie.

Kokla Chhapaki

Kokla Chhapaki (KOHK-lah chih-PA-kay) is a fun game for a large group. Children in India have played it for many years. Children in other countries play versions of the game, too. In many parts of the world, the game is called Drop the Hankie.

What You Need

- six or more players
- a handkerchief
- scissors
- thread
- a marble

How to Play Kokla Chhapaki

1 Get the hankie ready.
(See box at right.)

2 Choose someone to be It.
Have the rest of the players sit
in a circle, facing each other.

3 If you are It, walk around
the outside of the circle while
holding the hankie. Pretend
to drop the hankie behind
each player.

4 At some point, actually drop
the hankie behind someone.
Then keep walking.

5 If you are a player
in the circle, feel behind you
for the hankie. (Don't look!
That's not allowed.)

6 If you feel the hankie
behind you, pick it up. Quick!
Chase It around the circle.
Try to tag It with the hankie.

How to Make the Hankie

- Cut a piece of thread.

- Put the marble into
the center of the
handkerchief and
wrap the cloth
around it.

- Tie the thread tightly
around the marble so
it can't fall out.

Turn the page to find out
who becomes the next It.

Who Is It?

If a player tags It, the game goes on with the same It. If It runs all the way around the circle without being tagged, he or she sits in the other player's place. Then the player with the hankie is It.

Seega

Seega (SEE-ga) is a board game that people have played for thousands of years. In fact, scientists have found Seega boards in the tombs of Egyptian mummies.

Seega is a little like checkers or chess. It takes good thinking and planning to win. So choose your moves carefully.

What You Need

- two players

- a game board (See page 14.)

- three buttons or beans for each player

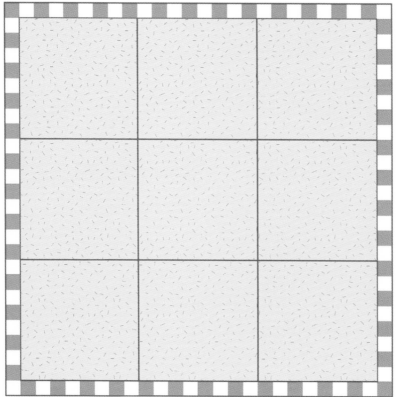

This is a Seega game board. You can play on this one or draw your own to use.

Seega Pieces

You can use coins, beans, buttons, or any small items as Seega pieces. Just make sure you know whose pieces are whose.

Setting Up the Board

Player 1's pieces

Player 2's pieces

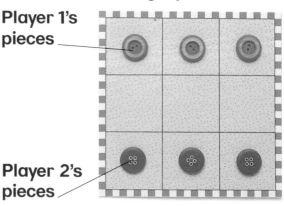

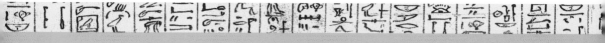

How to Play Seega

1 Each player places three playing pieces in a row on opposite ends of the board. The middle row should be empty. (See page 14.)

2 Decide who goes first. Players take turns.

3 On each turn, move your piece one or two squares in any direction (up, down, sideways, or diagonally). You can only move to an empty square. Do not cross a piece over any other piece.

4 The first player to move his or her pieces into a straight line wins. The line can run down, across, or diagonally. It can't be the same as the starting line.

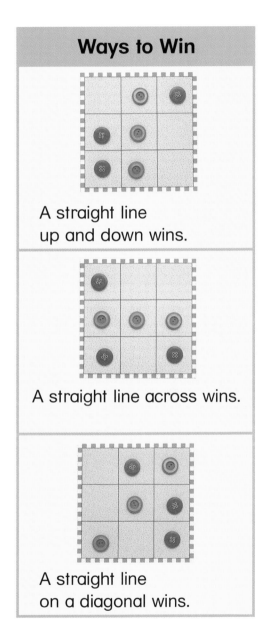

Ways to Win

A straight line up and down wins.

A straight line across wins.

A straight line on a diagonal wins.

More Games to Play

Country	What Children Play
Ghana	• Pilolo (a hide-and-seek game) • Da Ga (a tag game)
Mongolia	• horse races • Tonosh (a puzzle game)
Japan	• video games • bee-dama (marbles)
India	• Parcheesi (a board game)
Egypt	• Mancala (a board game)